Toast Lovers

POETIC VEGAN TOAST RECIPES

Cheryl Welch
Photographs by Charles Welch *(hey, he's my brother!)*

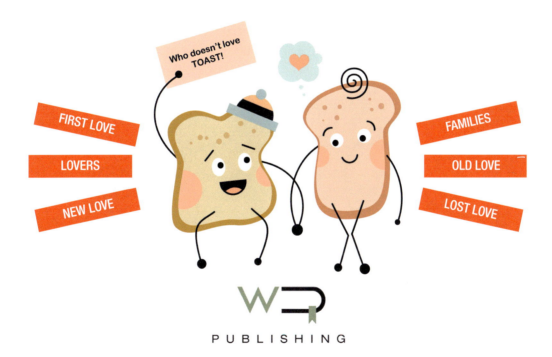

PUBLISHING

Try our toasty-cut shapes or just be "square!"
(it's about FUN, not perfection)

Savor this art-toastic look at love through imaginative poem-recipes, tasty photographs, and a healthy smattering of scrumptious toast facts.

We have created and designed the recipes, and taste-tested them for deliciousness (just ask our waistlines).

This toasty book is dedicated to those who love each other, themselves, and their neighbors. Let's "heel" the world.

1 We've listed ingredients and have included the action steps in lovely, loving, love poems.

2 Our recipes will delight the vegans in your life, but if it's not your bag, man ... substitute!

3 Toast becomes firmer if allowed to rest for a moment before topping.

4 We've cut some of our toasties into shapes *(tip: make a pattern out of paper)*. Try them out, or just be "square!"

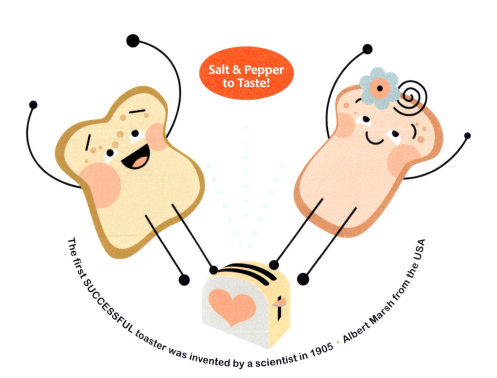

Salt & Pepper to Taste!

The first SUCCESSFUL toaster was invented by a scientist in 1905 · Albert Marsh from the USA

source: augustachronicle.com

Contents

Breakfast in Bed

You Had Me at Toast

Ingredients
makes two toasts

- Whole Grain Toast
- 4 tbsp Peanut Butter
- 4 Strawberry Slices
- 8 Blueberries
- 3 Green Grapes, Halved
- 2 tsp Crumbled
  Graham Crackers
- Swirl of Vanilla Icing
- Vegan Rainbow
  Sprinkles

TOASTY TIP:
We recommend whipping
up your own Vegan Icing
recipe (there are many
Online) as the ingredients
for such can be tricky

Morning devours us
Rising like bread toasted
Warming our large thoughts
    Our small talk
    Our days long with longing
Spreading fragrant and roasted
    Smoothing our shapes
Icing our words in soft
    And aching swirls

You whisper my name
Sing our song of strawberries
    Halved in half light
Making of our morning
    Fruitful hearts
    Sugared with envy
Among all who haven't
Spent their first words
    So sweet and lazy

sing

Slice of Life

Dropped in a vanilla pool of cool
Fresh fruit and cinnamon
Season your reasons

Swallow life's sweetness
In bits of friendship
Of families, of art and music

Adventure forward

Savor life's flavors
Feast on happiness
Expand its possibilities

By giving it away

Ingredients
makes two toasts

- Power Seed Toast
- 4 tbsp Vanilla Yogurt
- Slice and Chop a Peach
- Cinnamon
- Several Blueberries

The toaster was INVENTED IN 1893 Scotland by Alan MacMasters!

BUTT it only toasted one side of the bread

source: brignews.com

feast

Early Birds

Ingredients
makes two toasts

- Power Seed Toast
- 4 tbsp Vegan
  Cream Cheese
- 2 tbsp Chopped Chives
- 2/3 cup Sesame Sticks
- Few Shreds of Lettuce
- Sesame Seeds
- 4 Chickpeas

This is not a poem

This is a soft white cloud
    a bed of cut greens
    and seeded sticks
This is the tender nest
    of love birds
    unfurling wings
    beneath the sun's
    first rays

Encouraging their young
    to chance the day
    forward
This is a forever pair
    unprepared
    for forever
    for joyous worry

Witnessing the small
    artless flight of youth
Knowing that
    their own wings
    are wide enough
    to soften
    most landings

fly

Dream Date

Lost in thought
Our conversation
Lingers in music
Felt instead of heard

Blended in
Buttered apple
Smooth dates
And rolled oats

Laying In wait of a
Gentle coconut rain
Swirl of Icing
Crumbled sweetness

I daydream our night
As if tending a
Bright flower
About to open

Ingredients
makes two toasts

- Power Seed Toast
- 4 tbsp Apple Butter
  + 1 tsp Oats
- 4 Pitted Dates, Sliced
- Sprinkle of Coconut
- Swirl of Icing
- Crumbled Cookie

TOASTY TIP:
Use a lipstick tube top, or similar sized cap, to punch out the bubbles under the thought balloon

source: youkneadsourdough.com

dream

Banana Fan

Smashed and mixed
With oated grain
Bananas are the
Stuff of fame

Spiced, flaked
Topped with berries
Their fans are small, tall
Wide and hairy

The hero of each
(and every meal)
Bananas adore a
Spotlight steal

Ingredients
makes two toasts

- Whole Grain Toast
- 1 Mashed Banana
  + 1/4 cup Oats
- 1/4 cup Blueberries
- Pinch of Cinnamon
- Sprinkle of Coconut

The WORLD RECORD time to eat a slice of toast is 8.47 seconds

Anthony Falzon in 2014, he's my JAM!

source: guinnessworldrecords.com

adore

Pillow Talk

In our too small bed
We slice our day in
Cucumber and avocado
Smooth hummus
Peppered with heat

We

Whisper love words
Hold hands
Feeling a halved
Red heart between us
Making each of us

Whole

Our green blanket
Covering our cold
Warming our resisted

Sleep

Ingredients
makes two toasts

- Whole Grain Toast
- 4 tbsp Hummus
- 4 Avocado Slices
- 1 Cherry Tomato, Halved
- 2 Lettuce Leaf Blankies
- 4 Cucumber Slices
- A Few Red Pepper
  Flakes

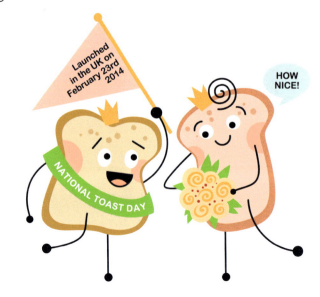

Launched in the UK on February 23rd 2014

NATIONAL TOAST DAY

HOW NICE!

whisper

Apple of My Eye

Ingredients
makes two toasts

- Cinnamon Toast
- 4 tbsp Apple Butter
- 2 Apple Slices, Halved
- 1 tsp Crushed
  Graham Crackers
- Dried Cranberries
- Cinnamon

We lay shaded
    Beneath apple blooms
    Anticipating their bounty

Recalling how we once
Spread their sweetness
On morning toast
    Sliced them crisp and tart
    Sprinkled them in
    Crushed graham flour
    Cinnamon

Seeding their center with
Cranberries

I take your hand

We turn our faces to look
Beyond our differences

Consider in silent minutes

If what was once

Can be again

consider

Let's Do Lunch

Afternoon Delight

Ingredients
makes two toasts

- Wheat Toast
- 2 tbsp Vegan
  Cream Cheese
- 2 tbsp Pumpkin Puree
  + 1 tsp Brown Sugar
- A Few Raisins
- Cinnamon
- Blueberries

TOASTY TIP:
This shape can
be easily cut using
kitchen shears

The sun
Up for hours
Lights the way
For all to discover
    Their paths

We toast their seeking
As we journey wild
Rising spicy
From our blanket
    Of white

Share dreams of
Blended pumpkin
    Sugar and raisins

Sweeten our morning
With berries

Feeling midday on backs
We become our own
    Destination

journey

Power Lunch

We crackle
The atmosphere
In this loud room
     of low murmurs, deals and handshakes

Dining on
Fragrant hummus
     flake-peppered, bright with seeds
We reach for the
Tip of the spear

Fingers almost touch

A bolt of light
Shocks the space
     we share between sky and earth

Ingredients
makes two toasts

- Rye Toast
- 3 tbsp Hummus
- 4 Spears Steamed Asparagus (some tips, and some chopped)
- Sesame Seeds
- Red Pepper Flakes

ANCIENT EGYPTIANS toasted bread over an open flame

DUDE! That's SO fire!

crackle

Tic Tac Mac

We bubble in warm water
        Until our elbows are
        Soft and smooth

Arise from our bath to
        Lie drained and shaken
        Our bed prepared
                Swirled together
                Creamy white
                Poured milk
        And mustard
                Shredding our sharpness
                Stirred and warm
                Spreading delicious

We make of our lives
        Dried and scattered fruit
        Game our future in
        Swallowed sunrises

Ingredients
makes two toasts

- White Toast
- 1/2 cup Cooked Macaroni
  + 1/4 cup Vegan Cheddar
  + 2 tbsp Vegan Mayo
  + 1 tbsp Soy Milk
  + 1/4 tsp Dijon Mustard
- Dried Tomatoes
- Green Olives

TOASTY TIP:
Gently warm your "mash-up" in a pan or microwave before spreading it on toast

You're TOAST!!!

bubble

A Corner Table

Ingredients
makes two toasts

- Rye Toast
- 4 tbsp Vegan
  Cream Cheese
- 2 tbsp Apricot Jam
- 1/2 Avocado
- Sesame Seeds

Cozied in soft white light
Feeling the only ones
In this space
      loud music
      violent laughter
      wild dancing

you
      cut cool and earthy
me
      citrus sharp
us
      feeling the seeds
      of something growing

An unlikely pair
Of fireflies drawn
To what may be
Our own demise

we
      kiss
      make it so

laugh

Toast-ada

Ingredients
makes two toasts

- Whole Grain Toast
- 6 tbsp Black Beans
- Dash of Chili Powder
- A Few Lettuce Shreds
- 2 tbsp Crumbled
  Tortilla Chips
- 2 tsp Salsa Topper

You are my favorite blend
    chili-sprinkled
    mashed beans
    chunky salsa

Spicy beautiful
Laid soft on our blanket
    in the sun

I complement your
    peppery edges

Offer cool sliced greens
    crumbled tortilla
    crackling crisp

Shaded at high noon under
    a low umbrella

We toast our differences
Share our strengths

Thrive in each other's
    shadows

thrive

Chips and Dip

Ingredients
makes two toasts

- Sourdough Toast
- 3 tbsp Cilantro Chili Sauce
- 1 tbsp Chopped Chives
- 2 tbsp Shredded Carrots
- Crumbled Veggie Chips
  + A Few for the
    "Dipping Chips"

Families gather
    Discuss the weather
        Favorite teams
            How children grow

Share differences
    Lightly spiced words
        Chive and carrot in
            Apparent contrast

Blend harmonious
    Around the little chips
        (off the old blocks)
            Who wrap us together

    Dipped in

      Praise

      Admiration

Enjoy the ultimate honor of
    Holding each other's
      Children

gather

My Little Chickpea

Ingredients

makes two toasts

- Wheat Toast
- 1/2 cup Mashed Chickpeas
  + 1/2 Stalk Diced Celery
  + 1 tbsp Vegan Mayo
  + 2 tbsp Raisins
- Curry Powder
- Slivered Carrots
- 2 Olives, Halved

Little one

My love for you is mixed
Of all things wonderful
As I recall your small face
    Covered in mashed peas
    In creamy white clouds
    Carrying handfuls of
    Celery and raisins
      Until they spill
      In careless forgetting

Spread in heartbeats
I watch you flutter by
    Filling my stomach with
    Beating wings

I binocular your flight
Through forests dusted in
    Golden yellow Fall
    Touching every heart
      Along the way

Hoping to be the flower
    Of your return

hope

Dinner for Two

Spring Rollin'

Spring rolls in
    shelled pods
    pulled from earth
    spread warm

Through the window
    slivers of mango
    a shredded root
    stripe the walls
    pattern our lives

Evening brings peace
    in souls satisfied

    pause

In grateful anticipation
    feeling the weight
    of small rains that
    drizzle our days
    seed our seasons

Ingredients
makes two toasts

- White Toast
- 4 tbsp Peanut Butter
- 1/2 Mango
- 1 Small Carrot
- 2 tbsp Peanuts
- Soy Sauce Drizzle
- Sesame Seeds

pause

Sweet Tato

Ingredients

- Whole Grain Toast
- 2 tbsp Sweet Potato
  + 1/4 Banana, Chopped
  + 1-1/2 tsp Brown Sugar
  + 1/4 tsp Vanilla
  + 1 tbsp Oats
- 2-3 Banana Slices
- A Few Dried
  Cranberries

TOASTY TIP:
Make your Sweet Potato
"Mash" ahead of time

My love

Know that you are
    complete and wondrous
A frantic blend of
    banana and sugar
    oats and vanilla
Spread wide in love
    admired by
    all you encounter

Cover your lonely hours
    in cranberries
    in friendship and poetry
    in music and travel
Use your broken
    your beautiful ruin
    to see the truth

That every break
Leaves you more whole

complete

Upper Crusty

When we are old
    beyond reason
We will rise to discover
Another chance
To know
    the chill of cool sauce
      the dicing of tofu
        of avocado
Having been spread
And scattered together
As we ourselves will have
Become one

We will make of our words
    a salad to top our day

Dressing it excited
    for another 24 hours
      to love each other

Ingredients
makes two toasts

- Wheat Toast
- 4 tbsp Vegan Mayo
- 2 tsp Crumbled Tofu
- 1/4 Avocado, Diced
- Bits of Lettuce
- 2 Tomato Slices
- Salad Dressing
  Drizzle

"Toast" is from the Latin word "tostum," meaning "to burn or scorch"

That BURNS me up!

rise

Breaking Bread

Ingredients
makes two toasts

- White Toast
- 1 Medium Potato
  + 2 tsp Vegan Butter
  + 2 tbsp Soy Milk
- 1/2 cup Cooked
  Green Beans
- Crispy Fried Onions

TOASTY TIP:
Gently warm your
"mash-up" in a
pan or microwave
before spreading it
on toast

We gather
Around a long table
    measured in missing
    felt in torn

We mash potatoes
Bathe them in the
    butter and milk
    of our youth

Remembering

Trimming the greens
Steaming them bright
    chopped and topped
Tossed in crisp new lives
    shared in mouthfuls of

    forgive

sorry

    love

forgive

Toast of the Town

Ingredients
makes two toasts

- White Toast
- 2 tbsp Vegan
  Cream Cheese
- 2 tbsp Raspberry Jam
- 5 Blackberries, Halved
- Vegan Rainbow
  Sprinkles

Here's to you
My long remembered
Good-natured friend
Cream of the crop

Spreading each day
In memory
In raspberry jam
In halved blackberries

You remain
Sliced and scattered
Into conversations
Into laughter and longing

I toast your love
Your benevolence
Your kindness
Your humor

Your beautiful mind
Forever sprinkled
In rainbows

remember

Pasta-bilities

Linguine nestled chicks
  Bathe in a light spray of
  Lemon and oil

Feather their nest with
  Bits of dried sun
Warm themselves in their bed of
  Vine-ripened softness

Sleep sweetly among scented herbs

Rise hungry

Find friendship beyond hunger
  Debate the possibility of love
  Beyond friendship

Ingredients
makes two toasts

- Wheat Toast
- 4 tbsp Marinara Sauce
- 3/4 cup Cooked Linguine
  + 1 tsp Olive Oil
  + 1/4 tsp Lemon Juice
- Sun-dried Tomatoes
- 1/4 cup Chopped Chickpeas
- Oregano

TOASTY TIP:
Spread the center of the toast with marinara sauce before forming the nest

Toss the linguine with oil and lemon before shaping into a circular nest

Toast was known as "TRENCHER" in medieval England

!

TRUE! It was used as a plate for serving other foods

source: edibleorangecounty.ediblecommunities.com

nestle

Bread Winner

Ingredients
makes two toasts

- Rye Toast
- 1 tbsp Dijon Mustard
- Sauté in 2 tsp Olive Oil
  + 1 cup Chopped
    Mushrooms
  + 2 cup Spinach Leaves
  + 2 tbsp Chopped Onion
- 1/2 Stalk Celery
- Thyme

TOASTY TIP:
Spread the toast with
mustard before topping

Make your Veggie Sauté
in advance

In gratitude
    We oil and heat
Sliced mushroom
    Spinach leaves

Watch them wilt
    Brown with onion
In time and thyme
    Sprinkled

Thankful

Spread the spread
    On a bed spiced yellow
Chop celery to top
    What is already

Perfection

We shy at our
    Good fortune
Chance meeting
    Dream our future

Success

meet

It's a Dessert Topping

Do Tella

serves one

Ingredients

- Raisin Toast
- 1/2 cup Melted Vegan Chocolate Chips
- 1/2 tbsp Crumbled Graham Crackers
- Dried Cranberries
- Chopped Cashews
- Icing

TOASTY TIP:
To easily melt chocolate chips, microwave them in 10-second rounds, stirring in between until smooth

1/2 cup Chocolate Chips yields approximately 2 tbsp of melted chocolate

These simple words
Speak my love for you

Kindness:
Filling my empty cup
With sweet

Melting:
Smoothing my hard edges
With your warm touch

Crush:
Remembering shared
Crackers and nuts
On a blanket
Under your cherry tree

Eyes:
Cranberry-iced
Reflected in the gaze
Of another

My cherished love
Lives quiet in my youth
Moves forward with me
Through time

cherish

Pop-Up Tart

We should not be surprised that love found us ready
Tapped our shoulders, caused us to turn
Wide eyes, open mouths

Love offered in soft swirls of cream and cranberry
Sweet juice of pears, cinnamon sprinkled
A falling of powder

We should not be surprised feeling warm surround us
In the everywhere of every day

Love has proved, regardless of our esteemed low
We are lovable and we love profoundly

Ingredients
makes two toasts

- Sourdough Toast
- 4 tbsp Vegan
  Cream Cheese
- 2 tbsp Cranberry Sauce
- 6 Pear Slices
- A Few Dried Cranberries
- Sprinkles of Cinnamon
  and Powdered Sugar
- Carrot Strips for
  "Surprise" Garnish

56

surprise

S'more Please

Ingredients
makes two toasts

- Raisin Toast
- 4 tbsp Peanut Butter
- 2 tsp Vegan
  Chocolate Chips
- 2 Vegan Marshmallows
  Sliced in Quarters
- 2 tsp Crushed
  Graham Crackers
- Cinnamon

Viewed from my heart I watch
    The future history of our children
    Blanketed against a slight chill
    Protected and held around
    A backyard campfire

Laughter-filled sparks lick the dark night
Little faces glow in the light of pure love

We now gather our adult selves
    Around a fireplace
Toast your memory in our best efforts
    In peanut butter
    In graham crackers
    In chocolate

In marshmallows soft with memory
Sweet with life

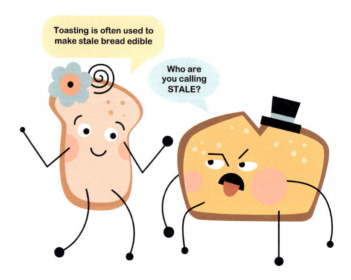

Toasting is often used to make stale bread edible

Who are you calling STALE?

protect

Blueberry Pie

simple is

as

simple does

as

is with toast

as

so with love

Ingredients
makes two toasts

- Raisin Toast
- 4 tbsp Vegan
  Cream Cheese
- 1/2 cup Blueberries
- 2 tbsp Cookie Crumbles
- Cinnamon

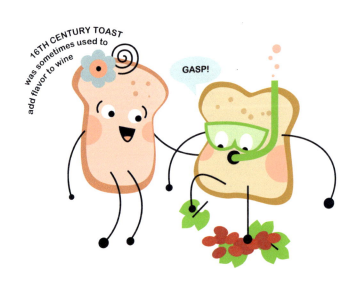

16TH CENTURY TOAST was sometimes used to add flavor to wine

GASP!

love

Be Twixed and Between

Ingredients
makes two toasts

- White Toast
- 4 tbsp Peanut Butter
- 2 tbsp Flaked Coconut
- Drizzle of
  Carmel Syrup
- 1 tbsp Vegan
  Chocolate Chips

In the between
	we shell ourselves
	roast and crush
	our envy

Spread our bed
	lay laughing as
	chocolate raindrops
	and sweet snowy
	flakes fall

Our pieces

Separated

	but no less loved

	connected by
	the space
	between our
	differences

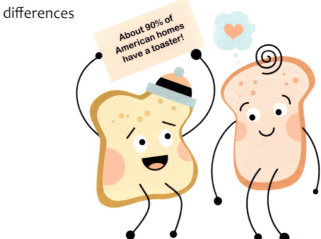

About 90% of American homes have a toaster!

goupstate.com/story/news

connect

Sweet Dreams

You will feel me in dreams of

    Sweet cream and carrots
    Cranberries and Banana
    Spiced in trickery and foolishness

You will wake to touch me in

    Hopeful and future
    Secrets and too many pillows
    Tomorrows of sunsets

Ingredients
makes two toasts

- Raisin Toast
- 4 tbsp Vegan
  Cream Cheese
- Alternate Carrot Slivers
  and Dried Cranberries
- Banana Slice
- Cinnamon

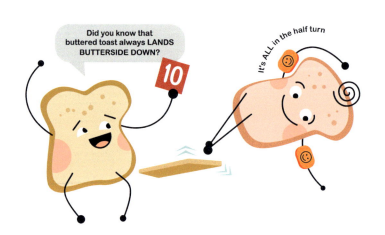

Remains of the Day

Ingredients
makes us all happy

- Love Received
- Making Memories
- Sharing a Meal
- Feeling Satisfied
- Finding Peace

Crumbs brushed from small faces
Shaken into the wind
        from checkered tablecloths
Emptied from paper bags
        landing on indifferent shoes
        feeding the birds

Sweetness licked from fingers
An empty jar having held the fullness
Of all that came before
        spreading thin a life
        that it may be filled again
        with friendship shared
        love sold without a price tag

Time savored in its passing
        toasting what is remaindered
        at the end of the day

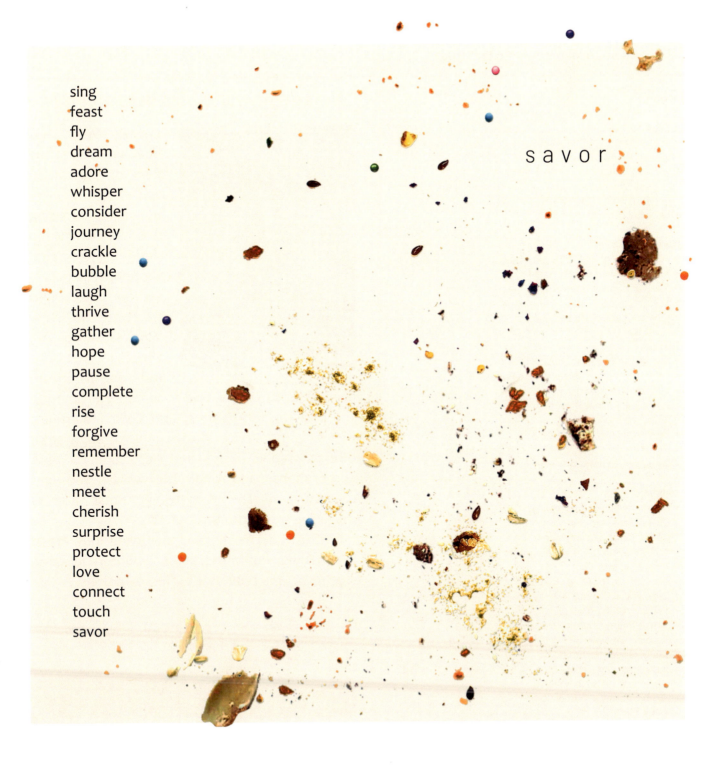

sing
feast
fly
dream
adore
whisper
consider
journey
crackle
bubble
laugh
thrive
gather
hope
pause
complete
rise
forgive
remember
nestle
meet
cherish
surprise
protect
love
connect
touch
savor

s a v o r

We used these products in our recipes!
All found at Local Grocery Chain Stores

Breads
- Avocado Street Bakery, Sourdough
- Dave's Killer Bread
  - 21 whole grains and seeds
  - 100% Whole Wheat
  - Power Seed
  - Raisin the Roof
  - White Bread Done Right
- Oroweat, Russian Rye

Non-Dairy "Dairy"
- I Can't Believe its Not Butter, Vegan
- Kite Hill, Cream Cheese, Plain
- Silk Dairy Free, Vanilla Yogurt
- Silk, Organic Soy Milk
- Violife, Cheddar Shreds

Spreads
- 365 Whole Foods, Pumpkin Puree
- Farmer's Market, Sweet Potato Puree
- Pacific Coast Selections
  - Creamy Peanut Butter Spread
  - Raspberry Preserves
- Signature Select, Apple Butter
- Signature Select, Wholeberry Cranberry Sauce
- Smuckers, Simply Fruit, Apricot

Toppings
- Alternative Baking Company,
  Outrageous Oatmeal Raisin Cookie
- Bitchin' Sauce, Cilantro Chili
- California Sun-Dry, Sun-Dried Tomatoes
- Enjoy Life, Mini Chips
- French's, Crispy Fried Onions, Original
- Good Food, Organic Date Syrup
- Nabisco, Grahams Original
- Nature Valley Granola, Protein
- Nosoya Plantspired Tofu Baked, Sesame Ginger
- Sabra, Classic Hummus
- Terra, Real Vegetable Chips
- Trader Joe's, Marshmallows
- Walden Farms, Caramel Syrup
- Wilton Sprinkles, Rainbow Nonpareils

"Never cut your bangs before coffee."

Cheryl Welch has been working in the field of illustration and design for over 40 years, including five years in Chicago designing packaging for Kenner Toys.

She has held positions in New York as Senior Art Director for the in-house art studio at American Express, and as in-house Promotion Art Director for *Parents*, and *Child* Magazines. Her own full-service studio, 1996 through 2022, offered graphic design and illustration for both corporations, and small businesses. She was co-editor at *The Wormwood Press* literary magazine from 2010 through 2021.

Cheryl currently runs an Online Indy Press, *Welch Design Publishing*, acting as writer, designer, illustrator, and publisher for her own titles.

Please look for Cheryl's poetry books, children's books and greeting card collections at the link below

welchdesignpublishing.com

Made in United States
Troutdale, OR
07/14/2024

21210614R00043